YOU GOTTA ASK

The Leader's Guide

Jon and Pam Strain
with Scott Greco

You Gotta Ask
The Leader's Guide
By You Gotta Ask, Inc. © 2021

The publisher of this book supports copyright. Copyright fuels creativity, encourages diverse voices, promotes free speech, and creates a vibrant culture. Thank you for buying an authorized edition of this book and for complying with copyright laws by not reproducing, scanning, or distributing any part of it in any form without permission. You are supporting writers and allowing authors to continue to publish books.

While the publisher and authors have used their best efforts in preparing this book, they make no representations or warranties with respect to the accuracy or completeness of this book and specifically disclaim any implied warranties or merchantability or fitness for a particular purpose. No warranty may be created or extended by sales representatives or written sales materials. The advice and strategies contained herein may not be suitable for your situation. You should consult with a professional where appropriate. The stories and interviews in this book are true although the names and identifiable information may have been changed to maintain confidentiality.

The publisher and authors shall have neither liability nor responsibility to any person or entity with respect to loss, damage, or injury caused or alleged to be caused directly or indirectly by the information contained in this book. The information presented herein is in no way intended as a substitute for counseling or other professional guidance.

Unless otherwise noted scripture quotations taken from the (NASB®) New American Standard Bible®, copyright © 2020 by Lockman Foundation. Used by permission. All rights reserved. www.lockman.org

Cover Concept and Logo Design: Tyler Penner Design
Cover and Interior Design: Fusion Creative Works, FusionCW.com
Lead Editors: Megan Terry and Heather Goetter
Book Production: Aloha Publishing

Softcover ISBN: 978-1-7365901-1-9

Published by: You Gotta Ask, Inc

CONTENTS

How to Use The Leader's Guide	7
The Detailed Leader's Guide	**13**
Optional Warm-Up Session	15
Session 1: Intro and Chapter 1	19
Session 2: Chapter 2	23
Session 3: Chapters 3 and 4	27
Session 4: Chapters 5 and 6	31
Session 5: Chapters 7 and 8	35
Session 6: Chapters 9 and 10	39
Session 7: Chapters 11 and 12	43
Session 8: Chapters 13 and 14	47
Session 9: Chapters 15 and 16	51
The Simplified Leader's Guide	**55**
Session 1: Chapters 1 and 2	57
Session 2: Chapters 3 and 4	61
Session 3: Chapters 5 and 6	63
Session 4: Chapters 7 and 8	67
Session 5: Chapters 9 and 10	69
Session 6: Chapters 11 and 12	71
Session 7: Chapters 13 and 14	73
Session 8: Chapters 15 and 16	75
The Open-Book Leader's Guide	**77**
You Gotta Ask Open-Book Quiz	84
Resources	87
About the Authors	89

HOW TO USE THE LEADER'S GUIDE

You Gotta Ask: The Leader's Guide is meant to help individuals lead discussion groups through the content of *You Gotta Ask* to help them apply the concepts and gain courage in their evangelism.

You Gotta Ask is about using compelling questions to create meaningful conversations that steer people toward Christ. The exercises in the book are intended to help readers practice asking the Platinum Question and get them thinking deeply about the concepts. Approaching these concepts as a group can be incredibly effective at helping readers learn from experience as they listen to each other's thoughts and stories, practicing empathy, and listening.

In our experience, a group discussion setting gives participants support and encouragement on their journey to becoming better witnesses for Christ and shows them how everyone has deep questions about God and life. It also provides accountability and a safe space to practice the exercises in *You Gotta Ask*, getting them to take action rather than simply digesting the information they read. Perhaps most importantly, participants learn to share their experiences as they gain courage through hearing each other speak.

With *The Leader's Guide*, you're equipped with three styles of discussion to help you direct a group through weekly, bi-weekly, or monthly discussions about the concepts of *You Gotta Ask*. These groups can be customized to your preferences and needs, but an ideal group would be composed of 3-14 participants. This number ensures that people can participate.

We recommend hosting bi-weekly sessions, which gives people enough time to read the content and complete any assignments you might give them. If you want to meet every week, do so knowing that you'll need breaks as people won't likely be able to attend every week. Flexibility is important. If you're limited on time, focus on the first eight chapters of *You Gotta Ask*, which are the core of the book. Take your time with them and adjust as needed.

Discussion groups for *You Gotta Ask* can be organized as part of an established group, or can be created anew. Everyone who comes should be prepared to listen and learn from each other.

As you read *The Leader's Guide*, keep in mind the kind of discussion group you want to run. In this guide, we provide three styles of discussion groups you can follow or adapt. Which style is best for you depends on your personal experience and comfort level leading discussions, your personal leadership style, and the people in your group.

THE DETAILED LEADER'S GUIDE

The first is a structured, detailed approach, including preparation steps, questions, guidance on running meetings, and homework assignments. This guide is excellent for first-time discussion leaders and people who prefer a more structured style. It is best used with a group of believers who want to become better evangelists using compelling questions. With this method, participants will read a couple of chapters each week and discuss what they've read using the questions provided in the leader's guide.

THE SIMPLIFIED LEADER'S GUIDE

The second is a less structured approach consisting of simple discussion questions. These are meant to expand on the questions and exercises in the *You Gotta Ask* book. Members will read a couple of chapters each week and meet to discuss their thoughts and experiences as they begin to try using the compelling questions in their own evangelism. This style is best suited to more experienced discussion leaders or those who prefer a less structured approach, following the conversation wherever it leads and being flexible to adapt to the topics that arise.

THE OPEN-BOOK LEADER'S GUIDE

Finally, the simplest way you can run a discussion group is to just use the questions in *You Gotta Ask*. While *You Gotta Ask* was written to help believers share their faith, the concept can also be used to help seekers explore questions about God and life. If you're interested in running a discussion group focused on seekers, we recommend focusing on the series of questions in *You Gotta Ask*, starting with the Platinum Question. Give everyone an opportunity to share their answers, interact with each other, and just listen. Watch for open doors, but don't interject. Personal questions that come up can also be addressed in this kind of group. Take the time to drill in on topics that tend to arise out of this type of group, such as the question of evil. This can also be a valuable exercise in a mixed group of believers and seekers.

When choosing people to invite to your discussion group, it's important to pray and make connections with the people you want to attend the group. Meet each one where they're at and tell them how they might benefit from it.

Before you begin your discussion group, read the entirety of *You Gotta Ask*, complete the exercises, and take notes on things you'd like to bring up. Read the *Leader's Guide* and determine which approach you'll use—or dip into all three—taking notes in the spaces provided about your own answers to the questions and topics you think might arise.

TIPS FOR LEADING DISCUSSION GROUPS

Below are some tips based on what we've learned from hosting discussion groups.

- If you've invited someone and they haven't responded, don't assume they aren't interested. You sometimes have to pursue someone, as their lives are busy and they need to be reminded.

- State your ground rules. Ensure that everyone recognizes the discussion group is a safe place, and what is shared is confidential. Your purpose is not to bash other perspectives, view points, or religions, but to create a place of learning. The golden rule is the ground rule.

- Encourage the relational aspect of the group. Have fun and engage in small talk. The discussion ideally should be between 45 minutes and an hour, but it's important to schedule time for small talk and getting to know one another. We recommend setting aside at least 90 minutes for a whole session.

- Watch the energy of the room. What excites and motivates people? Take more time to focus in on those topics. Similarly, sense when people are getting worn out and be ready to wrap things up.

- As the leader, practice and model what *You Gotta Ask* is about—empathetic listening. Your key role is to listen and facilitate discussion. Don't talk too much, but don't let other people dominate either, or sit too quietly. Your job is to let people be heard.

- You can overwhelm a fire with too much fuel and not enough air. Don't give people more information or more questions than they can handle at once. When a new topic arises, give it room to breathe and let people speak freely.

- Participants need to know that you care and that you're listening. Adapt your questions to what arises in the conversation. This is especially important in the beginning, when people may still be hesitant to speak. They will eventually start to ask their own questions, but it usually takes a while.

- If somebody is sharing a question or story, take notes so you can remember to follow up on it during the next meeting or ask how things are going with them. It also gives you an opportunity to pray for the people they've mentioned, their situations, and their questions.

THE DETAILED LEADER'S GUIDE

By Scott Greco

For leaders who prefer to have structure and resources, this guide contains detailed instructions to help you lead your discussion group. There is still room for creativity and we encourage you to adapt it to your own preferences and needs. This guide is best used with a group of believers, whether that's an established church group, bible study, or a group of individuals who wish to grow in their faith and their witness.

If you're someone who needs to think things out well in advance, this style should work well for you. Similarly, if you're not experienced in leading discussion groups, the structure of this style can be helpful.

We recommend you work through the questions ahead of time and write down your own answers. Think through how you might adapt the questions or the structure of the meeting to fit your personal style and the group you're working with—don't try to do something that doesn't make sense to you.

This style of discussion group begins with assignments to prepare both you as the leader and your group for the coming meeting. It also gives a structure for the meeting, as well as discussion questions and homework assignments for the following meeting. Feel free to use as much or as little as you want and adapt to what you believe will work best for your group.

OPTIONAL WARM-UP SESSION

PREPARATION:

Have your group participants complete the following exercises prior to the meeting.

> To introduce ourselves to each other, prepare to share the highlights of your life story in exactly five minutes. We will set a timer to heighten your internal story-editor and to stay focused on what's most important. Because it's difficult to fit everything you want to say into such a short time, please rehearse. Segment your life into the following periods: Birth to 12 years old, 13 to 21 years old, 22 to 30 years old, and 31 years old to the present. In these four segments, speak briefly about the people, events, or other memories that have most shaped you as the person you are today. Please spend more time on explaining the key people and events rather than providing a long list.
>
> While each individual is sharing, the rest of us will note points of common ground that we identify in each story. Please share only what you are comfortable with sharing, and know that our group is committed to maintaining the safest of environments for all of us to share and grow.
>
> Pray that God would begin developing your ability to identify common ground during discussions with others.

OPENING EXERCISE:

Start the meeting with quick group member introductions. Have each member share their name and why they chose to join the group.

Explain the ground rules for the group.

Explain the rules and purpose of the life story introduction exercise. Remind everyone to take notes when they identify an element of common ground, and ensure that they have paper and writing instrument to take notes. Determine who will keep time so that the exercise stays on schedule.

Ask for volunteers to begin sharing, or offer to go first. Thank each person for sharing.

REFLECTION QUESTIONS

What did you think? What are some generalizations that you can pull from this exercise?

. . . .
. . . .
. . . .
. . . .
. . . .
. . . .

Here are a few common observations people make:

- You can find common ground in anyone's story
- It is easier to share your story in a place of safety
- People really enjoy telling their story, even if they are shy or introverted
- It is almost impossible to not have follow-up questions you want to ask because of the five-minute limit

CONCLUSION

Conclude with sharing prayer requests and a time of prayer together.

Provide a summary of the homework for the next lesson, and remind them when prayer requests will be sent out.

Socialize and share how grateful you are to have this group to walk through this study with.

HOMEWORK

Read the introduction and Chapter 1 of *You Gotta Ask*.

INTRO AND CHAPTER 1

PREPARATION

Read the Introduction and Chapter 1 of *You Gotta Ask*.

Pray that God would open the group's hearts and minds to the approach offered in *You Gotta Ask* and provide everyone with the boldness to put the tools into action over the coming weeks.

OPENING EXERCISE

Ask everyone to anonymously write down their answers to the Platinum Question on post-it notes. Collect the post-it notes and randomly distribute them to the group. Take turns reading them aloud to each other.

Follow up with these questions:

- What are your thoughts after hearing these questions?
- Would we expect to get different questions from a group with different characteristics and dynamics than our group?

CHAPTER 1 REFLECTION QUESTIONS:

What was your first impression after you read the Platinum Question for the first time? Were you overwhelmed with thought? Have you had a question like this for God for a long time?

. . . .

. . . .

. . . .

What do you think are the most asked questions?

....
....
....
....

The top three frequently asked questions are these: Why is there evil and suffering? What is my purpose? How am I doing in God's eyes?

Why do you think these are most asked?

....
....
....
....
....

What does someone's answer to the Platinum Question tell us about that person?

....
....
....
....
....

What did you think about Jon's "watch this" story in Chapter 1? Does his approach seem natural and easy, or do you think you would struggle to replicate it?

....
....
....
....
....

Do you have any hesitation or fear about using the You Gotta Ask method? If so, why?

....
....
....

Do you think you could ask the Platinum Question this week? Why or why not?

....
....
....

CONCLUSION

End the meeting with a challenge to participants to present the Platinum Question to someone this upcoming week—bonus points to those who offer the question to someone they've never met.

Share prayer requests and spend time praying for each other.

HOMEWORK

Read Chapter 2 "Why this Question?"

Ask the Platinum Question to someone

CHAPTER 2

PREPARATION:

Read Chapter 2

This week's study asks a number of deep questions. Consider sending these out before the meeting so that the group members can think about them beforehand:

- When was the last time that you felt judged or misunderstood by someone else who did not understand the broader context of your life?

- Why are you a believer?

Pray that God would continue to open the group's hearts and minds to the approach offered in *You Gotta Ask* and provide everyone with the boldness to put the tools into action over the coming weeks.

OPENING EXERCISE

Ask participants to share the last time they felt judged or misunderstood by someone else who did not understand the broader context of their life.

CHAPTER 2 REFLECTION QUESTIONS:

You Gotta Ask mentions that listening well allows us to identify barriers to faith. The three barriers it identifies are emotional, intellectual, and volitional. Let's explore these three barriers to faith.

Why are you *still* a believer? What is different or the same now from when you first became a believer?

. . . .

. . . .

. . . .

Examine each of the barriers to faith using the following questions.

Emotional barrier:

What emotional barriers have you experienced or have you seen in family and friends? Read Romans 12:15, James 1:19, and Proverbs 17:17.

. . . .

. . . .

. . . .

How do we help others overcome emotional barriers?

. . . .

. . . .

. . . .

Intellectual barrier:

What questions have you been asked about your faith or Christianity that were difficult to answer? Read 1 Peter 3:15.

. . . .

. . . .

. . . .

How can we effectively respond to questions about God, the Bible, Christianity, and our faith?

. . . .

. . . .

. . . .

Volitional:

What were the natural barriers in your life before you came to faith?

....
....
....
....

Read Ephesians 2:1-3 and 2 Corinthians 4:3-4. What do these verses tell us about our fallen nature?

....
....
....
....

How can we respond to those struggling with a volitional barrier?

....
....
....
....

Now that we have studied the three barriers to faith, how can we be safe listeners?

....
....
....
....

What were your thoughts after reading Jon's Adventure Dinner story?

....
....
....
....

CONCLUSION

End the discussion with a challenge to circle back with the person or people that the group presented the Platinum Question to last week and ask them the follow-up question, "So out of all of the questions you could have asked, why this one?"

Share prayer requests and spend time praying for each other.

Socialize and share how grateful you are to walk through this study with this group.

HOMEWORK

- Read Chapters 3 and 4

- Ask the Platinum Question to someone.

CHAPTERS 3 AND 4

PREPARATION:

Read Chapters 3 and 4

Pray that God would continue to open the group's hearts and minds to the approach offered in *You Gotta Ask* and provide everyone with the boldness to put the tools into action over the coming weeks.

OPENING EXERCISE

What are the primary distractions in our lives that keep us from thinking deeply?

．．
．．
．．

CHAPTER 3 REFLECTION QUESTIONS:

What is the last personal question you had or received from someone else that you took the time to find an answer?

．．
．．
．．

What is the difference between competence and arrogant certainty?

．．
．．
．．

How do we exhibit humility through openness and curiosity while remaining committed to being competent in the subject matter?

．．

．．

．．

．．

Have you ever had this humility modeled by someone else for you? Explain.

．．

．．

．．

．．

What was so powerful about Pastor Mike's question and response to Jon's answer in this chapter's story section?

．．

．．

．．

．．

CHAPTER 4 REFLECTION QUESTIONS:

Outside of this community group, how do you satisfy your need for community and the mentorship of others, to feel connected, and to explore compelling questions outside the "bunker of your own mind"?

．．

．．

．．

Who is the mentor who has been most impactful to you? Why?

．．

．．

．．

Who could you invite to coffee or lunch to hear their story?

What is one area of your life where you could use a mentor right now?

CONCLUSION

End the discussion with a challenge to circle back with the person or people that the individuals in the group presented the Platinum Question to and ask them the follow-up questions, "How would you answer your question for yourself right now?" and "Do you know anyone who could guide you, or a resource you can consult, to find an answer to your question?"

Share prayer requests and spend time praying for each other.

HOMEWORK

Read Chapters 5 and 6

CHAPTERS 5 AND 6

PREPARATION:

- Read Chapters 5 and 6

- Pray that God would continue to open the group's hearts and minds to the approach offered in *You Gotta Ask* and provide everyone with the boldness to put the tools into action over the coming weeks.

OPENING EXERCISE

Do the *You Gotta Ask* open-book quiz as individuals on page 77. How well does everyone remember the six questions?

CHAPTER 5 REFLECTION QUESTIONS:

What was the last thing you asked God to reveal to you?

....
....
....

If God answered, how did you respond? If not, why do you think He was silent?

....
....
....
....

What stops us from asking God to answer our questions?

. . . .

. . . .

. . . .

CHAPTER 6 REFLECTION QUESTIONS:

Do you agree with Jon and Pam's assertion that people are "God-coded," that we intuitively know His attributes? Why or why not?

. . . .

. . . .

. . . .

. . . .

What attribute of God speaks to you most? Which is most important to you?

. . . .

. . . .

. . . .

Would you feel comfortable leading the "create a God" exercise? Why or why not?

. . . .

. . . .

. . . .

What did you think of Jon's discussion with Randy regarding everyone having a calling in life?

. . . .

. . . .

. . . .

CONCLUSION

Share prayer requests and spend time praying for each other.

HOMEWORK

Read Chapters 7 and 8.

Circle back with the person you asked the Platinum Question and ask them these follow-up questions:

- "Have you ever thought to simply and directly ask God your question? What have you got to lose?"

- "For you to be a praying person, what would you need God to look like? What attributes do you need God to possess? What moral perfections or superpowers would make God 'God' for you?"

Prepare a lead-in to the Platinum Question as directed in Chapter 7 of *You Gotta Ask*.

CHAPTERS 7 AND 8

PREPARATION:

- Read Chapters 7 and 8.

- Prepare your own lead-in to the platinum question as discussed in Chapter 7.

- Pray that God would continue to open the group's hearts and minds to the approach offered in *You Gotta Ask* and provide everyone with the boldness to put the tools into action over the coming weeks.

OPENING EXERCISE:

Share any opportunity you had (or passed up) to ask the Platinum Question. What kind of internal barriers did you experience deciding to ask or not to ask?

....
....
....

CHAPTER 7 REFLECTION QUESTIONS:

Why is it so powerful to use someone's name early in a relationship?

....
....
....

How good are you at remembering names? What techniques do you use to remember names?

....
....
....
....

Which of the three lead-ins (generic, brief, bold) that Jon offers resonated most with you?

....
....
....
....

Why is it important to ask permission and provide context prior to using these compelling questions?

....
....
....

Does anyone want to share the lead-in that they worked on for homework?

....
....
....

CHAPTER 8 REFLECTION QUESTIONS:

When you meet someone, what questions do you typically ask to initially get to know them?

....
....
....

SESSION 5

How long does it typically take you to hear their story?

....
....
....

Pam mentions three questions that she likes to ask people as she is establishing a relationship with them:

"Tell me your story."

"Tell me a little about what makes you, you."

"Tell me a little about your religious background."

What is your reaction to these questions?

....
....
....

How can you avoid being perceived as having an agenda?

....
....
....

What do you think of Pam's notion that most people are not rejecting Christ, but a poor caricature of Christianity?

....
....
....

Which technique (Jon's or Pam's) do you see yourself using in the future? Why?

....
....
....

CONCLUSION

Share prayer requests and spend time praying for each other.

HOMEWORK

- Read Chapters 9 and 10

CHAPTERS 9 AND 10

PREPARATION:

Read Chapters 9 and 10.

Pray that God would continue to open the group's hearts and minds to the approach offered in *You Gotta Ask* and provide everyone with the boldness to put the tools into action over the coming weeks.

OPENING EXERCISE

Teachers sometimes do an exercise with young kids where they ask them to put large rocks, small rocks, sand, and water into a large jar in any order they choose. If the kid puts the small rocks and sand in first, the large rocks typically won't fit in the jar. This exercise teaches prioritization, demonstrated by putting the large rocks in first, followed by the small rocks, then the sand, and then the water. Consider the "big rocks" that have sustained your faith and your hope to this point, and write them down.

Go around the group and share the "big rocks" in your jars of faith.

CHAPTER 9 REFLECTION QUESTIONS:

Read 1 Peter 3:14-17. When was the last time you intentionally thought about the hope that the Gospel provides us as believers?

. . . .

. . . .

. . . .

Jon offers at least four reasons to hope in Jesus: His claims were audacious, He offers amazing grace over a merit system, His claims are testable and verifiable, and He addresses real needs. Which of these reasons most resonates with you?

. . . .

. . . .

. . . .

If someone asked you why you have hope, what would your answer be?

. . . .

. . . .

. . . .

CHAPTER 10 REFLECTION QUESTIONS:

Read 2 Timothy 1:6-14. What fears still get in the way of sharing your hope as freely as you would like?

. . . .

. . . .

. . . .

Do you feel that this *You Gotta Ask* study has helped break down some of those fears that lead to paralysis in sharing your hope? How so or why not?

. . . .

. . . .

. . . .

Were you able to gain any inspiration or encouragement from Charlie's story in this chapter?

. . . .

. . . .

. . . .

Who has been a model or mentor for you for the process of sharing one's faith? How so?

....
....
....

CONCLUSION

Share prayer requests and spend time praying for each other.

HOMEWORK

- Read Chapters 11 and 12

CHAPTERS 11 AND 12

PREPARATION:

Read Chapters 11 and 12

Pray that God would continue to open the group's hearts and minds to the approach offered in *You Gotta Ask* and provide everyone with the boldness to put the tools into action over the coming weeks.

OPENING EXERCISE

Jon and Pam mention that people are spiritually hungry, needing a place of peace and rest. How do your nonbeliever friends try to find peace and rest in today's society?

. . . .
. . . .
. . . .
. . . .
. . . .

CHAPTER 11 REFLECTION QUESTIONS:

Read Genesis 3:6-13 and 2 Corinthians 5. Prior to reading, give each person responsibility for one of the seven barriers (guilt, shame, fear, separation, blaming others, being blamed, and death) and ask them to listen for the barrier in Genesis, as well as Paul's encouragement to overcome that barrier in 2 Corinthians 5. Go around the group and share what each person captured about their assigned barrier.

Guilt:

....
....
....

Shame:

....
....
....

Fear:

....
....
....

Separation:

....
....
....

Blaming others:

....
....
....

Being blamed:

....
....
....

Death:

. . . .

. . . .

. . . .

Going back to our opening exercise, how can we be part of God's process of offering and providing peace and rest for nonbelievers?

. . . .

. . . .

. . . .

CHAPTER 12 REFLECTION QUESTIONS:

Chapter 12 of *You Gotta Ask* states, "We are hard-wired for truth, living as if truth can be known." How do you approach sharing what you know to be true in a post-modern society that believes truth is self-defined?

. . . .

. . . .

. . . .

Tim Keller said, "Tolerance isn't about not having beliefs. It's about how your beliefs lead you to treat people who disagree with you." What does "tolerance" mean to you?

. . . .

. . . .

. . . .

How do you, in a practical way, try to live out the type of tolerance you've defined? Do you have any stories you would like to share?

. . . .

. . . .

. . . .

Read Hebrews 11:1 and 12:1-3. How do we share hope and truth with a society that can scoff at the idea of faith in something unseen?

. . . .

. . . .

. . . .

CONCLUSION

Share prayer requests and spend time praying for each other.

HOMEWORK

- Read Chapters 13 and 14

CHAPTERS 13 AND 14

PREPARATION:

- Read Chapters 13 and 14

- Pray that God would continue to open the group's hearts and minds to the approach offered in *You Gotta Ask* and provide everyone with the boldness to put the tools into action over the coming weeks.

OPENING EXERCISE:

In the story part of Chapter 13, Jon gave a brief description of how he applied the Seven Truth Tools to his answer to the Platinum Question, his question for God. Together, let's do the same exercise on one of your own questions for God. Who would like to offer their question for exploring?

....
....
....

CHAPTER 13 REFLECTION QUESTIONS:

Which of the Seven Truth Tools is your "go to" source of revealing truth in your life? Are there combinations that you typically use? Are there any that you do not typically use?

....
....
....

What groups do you belong to where you can explore God and life questions?

. . . .
. . . .
. . . .

How has God communicated truth to you most powerfully in your life so far? Has His method changed over time?

. . . .
. . . .
. . . .
. . . .

CHAPTER 14 REFLECTION QUESTIONS:

Read John 10:1-21. From this passage, what is the prerequisite for hearing Jesus's voice?

. . . .
. . . .
. . . .

What was your reaction to the round pen story?

. . . .
. . . .
. . . .

How has God been a round pen handler for you in life? Has anyone else been a round pen handler for you?

. . . .
. . . .
. . . .
. . . .

SESSION 8

How do you go about discerning what God is saying to you? Do you have someone who can help you sort out His messages?

....
....
....

What can we take from the round pen example when it comes to our use of the six compelling questions with nonbelievers?

....
....
....

CONCLUSION

Share prayer requests and spend time praying for each other

HOMEWORK

Read Chapters 15 and 16

CHAPTERS 15 AND 16

PREPARATION:

Read Chapters 15 and 16.

Build your "definition" of the Gospel in 25 words or less.

Pray that God would continue to open the group's hearts and minds to the approach offered in *You Gotta Ask* and provide everyone with the boldness to put the tools into action.

OPENING EXERCISE
- Spend time reflecting on the overall journey we have been on through the past eight sessions:
- Finding Common Ground
- Paralysis of Fear
- Platinum Question
- Five Additional Questions
- Approaches
- Researching God
- Fear Barriers
- Truth Tools
- Listening to God

Are there any topics people still have questions about? Have any new thoughts or experiences arisen?

CHAPTER 15 REFLECTION QUESTIONS:

How do you invite God to speak to you?

....
....
....

How do you test what you are hearing?

....
....
....

Are you excited to get questions in return after asking your compelling questions?

....
....
....

CHAPTER 16 REFLECTION QUESTIONS:

What definition did you come up with for the Gospel? Have everyone share.

....
....
....

Pain, purpose, personhood, and performance are some of the most common topics the six compelling questions bring up. Which have you seen others struggle with the most?

....
....
....

SESSION 9

How has your view of sharing the Gospel changed over the course of this study?

. . . .

. . . .

. . . .

CONCLUSION

Share prayer requests and spend time praying for each other.

THE SIMPLIFIED LEADER'S GUIDE

By Pam Strain

This style of group discussion is best for a leader who prefers a flexible approach and likes to follow conversations as they naturally flow. It is more focused on the people and allowing the interpersonal dynamics to develop. Pam created this guide based on what works best for her. She thrives on interaction with people and prefers less structured conversations.

This guide is intended to help believers explore and become more confident in using compelling questions in their evangelism. To best use this leadership style, don't force discussion around any particular topic. Follow the energy of the participants and what they're most excited about. Write your own questions based on what you're interested in hearing.

Because there is less structure in this approach, we suggest preparing yourself for each meeting by immersing yourself in the text enough that you feel confident in what you're talking about before you go into the meeting. It's important to be willing to adapt. It can be effective to use your own personal examples to encourage discussion around a particular question, and we recommend writing these in the note space to prepare.

Use this guide as a jumping off point to get people to share what they want to talk about, then dive deep into those topics.

CHAPTERS 1 AND 2

PREPARATION:

Read Chapters 1 and 2 of *You Gotta Ask*.

OPENING QUESTION:

What is your biggest barrier in talking to others about spiritual things?

....
....
....
....

DISCUSSION QUESTIONS:

What's the point of this book? What are the author's hopes for you?

....
....
....
....

What is your answer to the Platinum Question? Why is it important for you to have a question for God?

....
....
....

Did you text or ask the Platinum Question this week? If so, how did it go?

．．．

．．．

．．．

What did you learn from the person you asked regarding their question for God?

．．．

．．．

．．．

How easy or hard was it to ask the question? Describe your experience.

．．．

．．．

．．．

．．．

What is the purpose behind Question 2: "Of all the questions you could have asked, why that one?"

．．．

．．．

．．．

．．．

Did you get to ask Question 2? If so, what insights did you gain from their answer?

．．．

．．．

．．．

．．．

．．．

SESSION 1

Who else comes to mind to whom you could ask the Platinum Question?

....
....
....
....

What have you learned in regard to evangelism and overcoming what paralyzes you?

....
....
....
....

CHAPTERS 3 AND 4

PREPARATION:

Read Chapters 3 and 4 of *You Gotta Ask*.

OPENING QUESTION:

Have you had an opportunity this week to overcome a fear barrier in initiating a conversation with someone? How did it go?

. . . .

. . . .

. . . .

DISCUSSION QUESTIONS:

Fear is the greatest problem all people face today. We are paralyzed by fear in our witness. Have you experienced any victory over fear in the past two weeks?

. . . .

. . . .

. . . .

How would you answer your own question for God? Is it hard for you to answer?

. . . .

. . . .

. . . .

Did you ask the third question to your person this week: "How would you answer the question for yourself?" If so, how did it go?

．．．
．．．
．．．
．．．

Were you able to ask any question to anyone recently? If so, how did it go?

．．．
．．．
．．．
．．．

Who do you have as a guide or mentor in your life?

．．．
．．．
．．．
．．．

Discuss isolation and how it has affected your relationships. What can we do to overcome this barrier?

．．．
．．．
．．．
．．．

Have you had an opportunity to invite someone to share their story? If so, how did you respond?

．．．
．．．
．．．
．．．

CHAPTERS 5 AND 6

PREPARATION:

Read Chapters 5 and 6 of *You Gotta Ask*.

OPENING QUESTION:

What are some compelling questions you have found to be useful?

....
....
....

DISCUSSION QUESTIONS:

Did you get to invite someone to share their story? If so, what response did you get?

....
....
....
....

What other significant conversations did you have?

....
....
....
....

What would cause you (or others) to *not* ask God your questions?

....
....
....

Does it feel risky to ask God your questions, or to ask someone else to ask? Why?

....
....
....

On page 47 of *You Gotta Ask*, you're encouraged to ask yourself, "Have I responded to the last thing God said to me?" What does this have to do with asking God something?

....
....
....

What did you glean from Randy's story?

....
....
....

Do you have any other insights from Chapter 5?

....
....
....

What's the purpose of the sixth question, the "create a God" exercise?

....
....
....

What was your first response to the "create a God" exercise?

. . . .
. . . .
. . . .

HOMEWORK

- Complete the "create a God" exercise with someone—your family or a friend.

CHAPTERS 7 AND 8

PREPARATION:

- Read Chapters 7 and 8 of *You Gotta Ask*.

OPENING QUESTION:

Share some insights you are learning about yourself as you "try on" this style of evangelism.

．．．
．．．
．．．
．．．

DISCUSSION QUESTIONS:

Did you get a chance to do the "create a god" exercise? What were the results?

．．．
．．．
．．．

What interesting conversations have you had lately?

．．．
．．．
．．．

Did you get to hear a story or tell a story? How did it go?

....
....
....
....

What "lead ins" work for you?

....
....
....
....

Give context for your questions. What is this and why is it important?

....
....
....
....

CHAPTERS 9 AND 10

PREPARATION:

Read Chapters 9 and 10 of *You Gotta Ask*.

OPENING QUESTION:

Have you had a chance to ask to hear someone's story? How did it go?

....
....
....

DISCUSSION QUESTIONS:

Did you have any opportunities to ask any compelling questions or hear a story?

....
....
....

On page 72 it says, "If we understand the gospel, we'll feel more prepared to present it to others and to defend it." Is this a new idea to you?

....
....
....
....

Why are you still a Jesus follower? What is your hope and why do you need Jesus? What are your top 3-5 bullet points about why you have hope?

. . . .
. . . .
. . . .
. . . .

What would happen if more people were prompted to ask God their questions?

. . . .
. . . .
. . . .
. . . .

On page 79 in *You Gotta Ask*, you were asked to guess the top 3 reasons people gave in a survey as to how they would live their life differently. Did you get any of the top 3 right? Why don't we risk more? How can we begin?

. . . .
. . . .
. . . .
. . . .

On page 82, what paralyzing factors do you relate to?

. . . .
. . . .
. . . .
. . . .

CHAPTERS 11 AND 12

PREPARATION:

- Read Chapters 11 and 12 of *You Gotta Ask*.

OPENING QUESTION:

Do you think people around you are spiritually open? Why or why not?

. . . .
. . . .
. . . .

DISCUSSION QUESTIONS:

What are your barriers to sharing the gospel? What keeps you from it? What paralyzes you? List them.

. . . .
. . . .
. . . .

Read 2 Corinthians 5. What in this passage motivates you to share the gospel? What kind of perspective should we have? Does it require a mindset shift?

. . . .
. . . .
. . . .

Do you believe people are spiritually hungry? How can you tell?

．．．

What is your takeaway from Chapter 12? Have you given much thought to absolute truth and its essential component to life?

．．．

How do we navigate the topic of absolute truth in a postmodern world?

．．．

What are the truth tools you use to verify the reality of your beliefs?

．．．

CHAPTERS 13 AND 14

PREPARATION:

Read Chapters 13 and 14 of *You Gotta Ask*.

OPENING QUESTION:

Describe some breakthroughs you have had since we've been discussing *You Gotta Ask*.

. . . .
. . . .
. . . .

DISCUSSION QUESTIONS:

Which truth tool is the hardest for you to use? How can you grow in using that tool more effectively?

. . . .
. . . .
. . . .
. . . .

How do we use these truth tools as a way of life?

. . . .
. . . .
. . . .

What has God been saying to you? How does he communicate with you?

．．．
．．．
．．．
．．．
．．．

How would you help someone discern if God is speaking to them?

．．．
．．．
．．．
．．．
．．．

CHAPTERS 15 AND 16

PREPARATION:

Read Chapters 15 and 16 of *You Gotta Ask*.

OPENING QUESTION:

Explore some ways you can segue to sharing the gospel. How do you know if someone is ready to hear it?

....
....
....

DISCUSSION QUESTIONS:

How do we hear God's voice? How do you hear it personally?

....
....
....

We need to be ready to share the gospel with people as we begin entering authentic conversations with them. Share your 25-word Gospel message you created on page 127 of *You Gotta Ask* with the group.

....
....
....

Will you consider taking the Romans Reading Challenge? Why or why not?

. . . .
. . . .
. . . .
. . . .

What are your top two takeaways or applications from our *You Gotta Ask* discussions?

. . . .
. . . .
. . . .
. . . .

What are you implementing into your life as a result of reading and discussing this book?

. . . .
. . . .
. . . .
. . . .

THE OPEN-BOOK LEADER'S GUIDE

By Jon Strain

The final style of discussion group leadership is to simply use the compelling questions in *You Gotta Ask* and follow the conversation wherever it leads. This could be structured by focusing on one question each week, or you could take more or less time on each question based on the responses from the group.

This approach to discussion groups is a great way to create a discussion group for seekers, helping them work through their questions. It creates a safe setting to help them discover their own thoughts and have an opportunity to air them. They need time, grace, humility, and empathetic listening, and this kind of discussion group is a great place to give them the response that they need.

There's also power in using a mixed group. There's no better way to see evangelism in progress. It energizes the believers like nothing else. But be aware that believers may drown out seekers by using too much in-speak (Christianese)—watch out for that. In addition to your ground rules, it's important to foster the attitude that we're all seekers.

This is one of the simplest approaches you can take to a discussion group, and you can spend a greater amount of time on each question. The questions are meant to help the group build curiosity. Take time to explore each participant's Platinum Question (their questions for God) as well as the compelling question sequence in Chapters 1-7. Sometimes these questions can be explored in smaller groups when two or more participants ask about the same topic, such as evil and suffering or life's purpose. The questions need to serve each person in the group by allowing them to fully explore their thoughts and feelings.

QUESTION 1

Assuming there is a God, and you could ask God anything, what would you ask?

QUESTION 2

So, of all the questions you could have asked, why ask this one?

QUESTION 3

How would you answer your question for yourself right now?

QUESTION 4

Do you know anyone who could guide you, or a resource you can consult, to find an answer to your question?

QUESTION 5

Have you ever thought to simply and directly ask God your question? What have you got to lose?

QUESTION 6

For you to be a praying person, what would you need God to be like? What attributes do you need God to possess? What moral perfections and superpowers would make God "God" for you?

YOU GOTTA ASK OPEN-BOOK QUIZ

Use this open-book quiz to help group members test their memory of the six compelling questions.

Complete the rest of each compelling question below.

COMPELLING QUESTION 1:

Assuming . . .

COMPELLING QUESTION 2:

So, . . .

COMPELLING QUESTION 3:

How . . .

COMPELLING QUESTION 4:

Do . . .

COMPELLING QUESTION 5:

Have . . .

. . . What have you got to lose?

COMPELLING QUESTION 6:

For . . .

. . . What attributes do you need God to possess? What moral perfections and superpowers would make God "God" for you?

RESOURCES

The resources below have been compiled to help you address topics that tend to arise in these discussion groups and when asking the six compelling questions.

There is no end to good resources, but these are good starting places. We briefly describe why we like each one.

Questioning God: Answers to Questions Worth Asking by John Hopper

> This book is written in a relational tone for a seeker/skeptic, but informative in content and style for a Christ-follower.

The Case for Christ by Lee Strobel

The Case for Faith by Lee Strobel

The Case for Creation by Lee Strobel

> This series, written by a former skeptic, approaches exploring the most-asked questions about God and life in an investigative journalist style.

More Than A Carpenter, Josh McDowell & Sean McDowell

> This book offers a brief and compelling explanation of what makes Jesus unique and why we can take his claims seriously.

I'm Glad You Asked, Larry Moody and Ken Boa

> Using logical flow charts, this book breaks down a dozen of the most asked and important questions..

The Reason for God: Belief in an Age of Skepticism, Timothy Keller

> This book appeals to a sophisticated audience, addressing common doubts seekers, skeptics, and even believers encounter about God.

ABOUT THE AUTHORS

ABOUT PAM

Pam is the Women's Director of You Gotta Ask, Inc, and serves in a mentoring role with women throughout the Treasure Valley. She co-founded LIFT (Live: Inspired. Fearless. Thriving.), which exists to create impactful, relational events and gatherings that welcome all women and encourage them to live inspired, fearless, and thriving lives. Pam loves creating safe places for women to openly explore tough questions and life challenges. Her favorite hobby is "soul sloshing"—talking with women over a cup of coffee about matters of the heart. She considers it a privilege to walk alongside women to help them discover and embrace who they are and their unique purpose.

ABOUT JON

Jon is the Executive Director for You Gotta Ask, Inc. Jon has generated "mission startups" including a Christian campus ministry at BYU in Provo, Utah; in Meridian, Idaho; and Search Ministries (national), in Boise. The theme of his ministries has always been relational evangelism, discipleship, and relational apologetics. Jon loves to train people's hearts and minds, exploring questions about God, life, and manhood. He pioneered the Adventure Dinner, which combines great food shared by interesting people exploring compelling ideas. Jon refuels in the foothills or along the river, hiking, running, walking, and mountain-biking with routine forays into hot yoga. He loves marking up books to glean ideas, but does his best thinking on the move. He enjoys great stories and learning from the life experiences of other people.

ABOUT SCOTT GRECO

Scott wrote The Detailed Leader's Guide section of this book. His view on relational evangelism was forever changed when he met Jon Strain in the summer of 2019. Since then, Scott has met weekly with the "Blue Sky Guys," a committed group of Jesus-followers. The group gathers to encourage one another and explore how they can reach their neighbors in the Treasure Valley. Before settling in Idaho, Scott and his wife, Karin, bounced around the country during a 20-year adventure in the U.S. Army as Scott served primarily as an attack helicopter pilot. Between combat tours, he discovered his love for teaching when he served as an instructor at West Point, his alma mater, and as the Professor of Military Science at the University of Tampa. As soon as the book, *You Gotta Ask*, was published, Scott led a group through a study and was excited to contribute in developing a leader's guide. Scott and Karin have three amazing and enjoyable kids. Scott also enjoys investing in the lives of young men and backpacking the mountains of Idaho especially when God allows these two passions to come together.

ABOUT YOU GOTTA ASK

You Gotta Ask is a nonprofit organization that creates relational settings to explore significant questions about God and life. It aims to bring seekers and nonbelievers one step closer to God through compelling conversations. It also provides tools to help believers share the Gospel through accessible questions that start easy conversations. Jon and Pam founded *You Gotta Ask* in the summer of 2020.

Notes

Notes

Notes

Notes

Notes

Notes

www.ingramcontent.com/pod-product-compliance
Lightning Source LLC
Chambersburg PA
CBHW081506040426
42446CB00017B/3424